How to improve your concentration

TRICKS AND MANEUVERS FOR CONCENTRATION AMPLIFICATION

OLIVER THOMPSON

ISBN: 1518833047
ISBN-13: 978-1518833045

CONTENTS

I think next books will also be interesting for you.

How to Organize Your Life

Memory Improvement

Getting Things Done

Introduction

How to improve concentration is the complete informational book that covers the main areas of concentration. From the beginning, understanding about what is the concentration is the most important besides learning the ways of improving it. Different aspects are also compared related to the concentration to provide the readers latest information about it. How to improve concentration is all about the practicing new and unique strategies along with many alternations in it. Explanation of the advantages and brain areas of concentration is also mentioned to add more knowledge about the attention ability.

This book is composed of five main chapters featuring with the interactive and interesting topics. The concentration is important for winning even very small task; without concentration, success could easily be turned into failure. The determination and dedication to accomplishing the task is regulated by the appropriate concentration. Thus it is the prior inevitable component that should be resisted throughout the task, no matter whether it is beginning or ending for catching the absolute success. Surrounding and routine can be distracters or assistors, if they are used wisely in any task; in concentration, usually it is seen that there are enormous hurdles but some ways are also included in this eBook to widen the range of choices for implementation in daily lives.

Some problems also occur while trying to pay entire focus on the existing task, how to cope with it and solve the problem within minutes is a must read text from this eBook. At the other end of the spectrum, the ways and tricks are enlisted to boost the memory and augment the concentration power by simply applying them to your lives. Exercises and meditation are also proven to be the concentration loving activity paralleled by leaving the positive effect on all over the body.

Thank you for downloading **"How *to improve concentration? Tricks and maneuvers for concentration amplification"*. This e-book is the complete tool for recharging the slow batteries of the mind with the latest and modified methods of improvising the concentration. At the end of each chapter, extraction of scientific facts from recent researches and bonus tricks are also added to increase the knowledge about the hidden factors of many useful activities and materials that we usually don't bother at all. From evaluation of the problem till the achievement of success, this eBook will help you in raising the ability, strength and skill of the concentration.

Chapter 1 – CONCENTRATION – THE OWNER OF SUCCESS

Focusing on one point, visualizing the object, recalling the past conversations and memorizing the things in a few minutes is all just because of the concentration. So, Concentration is the act of fixing an attention on one object or thing and discarding the surrounding's happenings. Concentration is all about the power of focus. If someone has good focus ability, then he would automatically have good concentration power as well; though, focus ability and concentration power are interrelated.

Engrossed for remembering the perceived information is the major factor of concentration. Besides distractions and disturbance in processing the information, the person's own level of saturation is very important. As it is the rule of nature, that every individual is different from each other whether in facial features or perspectives; so, how come concentration ability could be same for everyone. It is different, that's why you can memorize some objects quickly while others can't.

The area of interest is also important, because the choice of hobbies and hierarchy of habit is entirely dissimilar for everyone. Some people don't need to put too much effort for memorizing anything about their favorite topic in a fraction of minutes, but they may spend hours and hours to memorize a single paragraph of the book or any main point due to the disliking of the topic, this shows the concentration level is directly depends on the person's interested and indirectly depends on the uninterested objects. The greater the concentration on interested topic, the quicker memorization about the related topic and the more concentration on uninterested object, the more delayed learning process of the information. So, the concentration is not only depends on your mind's perceiving information capacity and ability; actually, it is the whole environment around you involves in maintaining and achieving proper attention.

SCIENCE BEHIND CONCENTRATION

Definitely, the brain controls the cognitive as well as motor functions. So, cognitive functions include the memory, decision making, thinking, learning ability and concentration, but the brain is divided into many different areas and zones, restricted to the specific task like our occipital area deals with the vision, similarly, our concentration is controlled and refined by the lateral intra-parietal cortex embedded in the parietal cortex.

After information is entered in the brain, it is firstly processed through the thalamus then stimulates the lateral intra-parietal cortex for alarming the brain to pay attention on the object, later on; this will activate the medial temporal area for attending or not attending the visualized information. If the response is positive that means the attention would be paid to the stimulus, but if rejected the stimulus is thought to be not effective in grabbing the attention of the person.

We all do this while noticing some things in the crowd and rejecting the other objects from the surrounding. If any injury to the brain is caused then it'll leave a negative impact on the chief monitors of the concentration and ultimately the concentration is impaired and the person has to face many embarrassing situations in future. Having the poor concentration power is not bad but doing nothing for solving it could be detrimental for pursuing in future.

ADVANTAGES OF CONCENTRATION

The concentration power is beneficial for perceiving any little amount of information because it'll lead to the development of memory about the targeted object. But some top main benefits of the concentration is described below

- Focus ability can be displayed

- Enhancement of memory

- Stronger Willpower development

- Self confidence improvement

- Control on the thoughts

- Ability of neglecting the not useful objects

- Visual ability utilization

- Perception quickly

- Hearing ability aggravation

- Psychic powers development

- Assists in accomplishing tasks like study or presentations

- Faster comprehension

CONCENTRATION IS THE ACCOMPLISHER OF GREAT TASKS

"The power of concentration manifests as focused attention and as a one pointed mind."

Without concentration, any task would be incomplete either it is the business meetings or family dinner. According to the Remez Sasson, when the is focused on one object, then the person will invest his all energy and inner power towards the stimulus and the attention will automatically developed towards the relevant object then ultimately, the task would be achieved with full success. This skill is inevitable for all individual but the ratio of usage could change among the individuals. If the concentration ability is not good, the thoughts in your mind would jump from one to another fatiguing your mind and at the end you won't make the proper decision about the relevant stuff.

No matter, on what level of saturation you are, the concentration ability must be improved to get your tasks and jobs done perfectly and faultlessly without spending too much time on the particular stimulus.

COMPONENTS OF CONCENTRATION

To sum up all the famous theories and studies, the concentration components are enclosed in three categories for the ease of the individuals.

- AS A FILTER

  Brain can concentrate on one object at a time that's why some information in our brain is accepted and some are rejected. This is the most common form of concentration that we all are using in our daily lives.

- AS A SPOTLIGHT
  Some people can easily pay attention to a variety of stimuli around them. This is because they are using their more efficiently and though responding and noticing more objects as the normal person can do. It also deals with the extent of concentration whether it is too long or too short.

- AS A RESOURCE

  Many psychologists proved that the human brain mostly behaves like the pools of information and processing like pool of information, pool of planning or pool of interest. It is believed that the larger the pool, larger the empty space and greater extent of information is processed; ultimately, achieving multi directional concentration on object.

"A recent study shows that playing effects- heavy, action oriented video games increases the visual attention system along with augmenting the concentration power"

Chapter 2 – IMPACT OF SURRONDING AND ROUTINE ON CONCENTRATION

Environment and daily routine do play vital role in increasing or decreasing the concentration; rather by distracting from the target or introducing disturbances in focusing the object. After all, you are living with your own scheduled routine and surroundings are unavoidable, but extraction of desired stimuli is difficult for concentrating on it and gives the appropriate response. By making small alterations in your daily routine and avoiding the unnecessary objects from the surrounding could be helpful in gaining the power of concentration over a short period of time.

NOISES

When trying to concentrate on an object or things, many noises are like friends of yours and others behaving like an enemy. Sometimes, the people couldn't pay their attention on the ongoing conversations and would confuse, if someone speak loudly in front of them, that'll unintentionally produce disturbance for the person to focus the object or to catch the conversation from the point left behind.

But some conversations are assistors in accomplishing the task, like learning by loud voices and listening the lesson verbally from anyone could easily help them to memorize the main point. Dealing with noise distracters isn't a big problem; there is a solution for every problem.

IMAGES AND TRACTS

Most of the people have the power of memorizing images rapidly while some others take more time to learn tracts and images. All this happens due to the concentration power, the little effort of concentration on the image could help in immediate capture of the object including the colors, styles and fonts in it, but it might confuse the others, whether they can only remember the color or style of the image.

 Scientists also discovered that the tracts and directions are very simple to learn for some people by just randomly looking around while walking or sitting in a vehicle but others can forget the same route even walking by it daily.

CALM AND IRRITANT ENVIRONMENT

The greater the environment is quiet and calm, the more focus can be paid for the targeted task but if the environment is too noisy and distractions are continuous, the concentration would be broken constantly. For that reason, calm environment is more relaxing because it enables to memorize without coping with the interrupting disturbances. However, studies also revealed that the intelligent people could efficiently deal with the irritant environment as compared to the calm environment due to the well trained concentration ability and power.

UNSYNCHRONIZED LIVING

The people who are living without any proper organization of the daily routine would affect more on the concentration ability. Perhaps, it could lessen the power of focus or strength to fix attention on any targeted object. The unsynchronized living won't also leave an impact on the concentration but overall it is a bad cup of tea. Unsynchronized daily routine could influence your mood and behavior too. Organizing your lives into a proper routine is very important for accomplishing each target of lives; either it is paying attention or succession of aims.

UNHEALTHY EATING AND DRINKING

Fizzy drinks and high carbohydrate diet are dangerous not only for your health but also for the memory and brain. Researchers discovered that the person eating the glucose rich substances in your diet can be the cause of brain function impairment on future. Smoking and alcohol abuse are one of the leading causes of altered concentration nowadays and the incidence is increasing day by day. But preventive measures can be helpful for dealing with the concentration impairing problems. You can't realize it in a daily routine, but the effects will start on when the unfriendly diet is increased.

SKIPPING THE BREAKFAST CAN WORSEN THE CONCENTRATION SKILL

While skipping breakfast, anyone couldn't realize that what the disastrous impact is leaving on their vital organs and systems. It is rightly *said to eat breakfast like a king, eat lunch like a common man and eat dinner like a beggar,* after waking up in the morning, our brain needs sufficient glucose to compete with the daily requirements of the nutrients and essentials, so boosting with the healthy breakfast is very important to spend the whole day efficiently and achieve the success in every task. For paying quicker concentration, your brain should be supplied with the full minerals and vitamins that we can get it by not skipping the breakfast.

DEHYDRATION AND CONCENTRATION

Drinking less water or natural fruit juices is one of the major causes of dehydration. Significantly, our body needs more water than the other essentials. So, if the quantity of water is not enough, our body's chief organs including brain, heart and kidneys will ultimately start dropping down and create an interruption while putting attention on the stimulus. Water is like a fuel for our body, if it isn't provided on time, the body will show bizarre response.

"Researchers from the Princeton University Neuroscience Institute published the result of current study that the clutter limits brain's ability to process information and helps in the distraction."

Chapter 3 – PARTICULAR PROBLEMS THAT FACED DURING CONCENTRATION

When trying to concentrate completely or engrossed in the targeted object, specific hurdles occurs that break the rhythm of concentration and eventually, you are unable to fix your mind's attention in one direction. Some people may overcome the rhythm and give the new start of the target rather others move here and there and forgetting totally about what they are actually doing or intended to do. Common issues are:

ABSORBANCE CAPACITY OF BRAIN IS FULL

Sometimes, it seems like you can't do more things or don't have the power to handle the big problems right away. It is just because of your absorbance capacity is full and now your brain needs some rest by easily leaving the task for a while. This issue is commonly seen in the student life when the study is prolonged and brain is bored from reading or learning about one thing constantly.

There is a limit set for each processing information in our brains, if we overuse it, the result will be end up by understanding nothing and just wasting the time. So, try to take a break from heavy study topics and review it to restore the energy of mind.

FIXING THE ATTENTION ON DISLIKED OR BORING TOPICS

The least the interest, the more focus should be paid to the topic. This is the human psychology that the stuff or topic which he doesn't like will ultimately show the disinterest towards it. It's quite difficult to be attentive in the lecture, presentation or even in the meetings, if the topic is boring; so, for dealing with this situation, you should say stop to combat it, try to focus on the topic as much as you can. Keep a notepad with you and write important points in it, it'll assist in maintaining the concentration throughout the meeting or lecture.

DREAMING WHILE CONCENTRATING ON A TOPIC

Usually, people start the day dreaming when sitting in front of the books and papers, and completely leaving the topic behind due to the interruption of future planning. The dreaming should be halted by reviewing yourself and preparing yourself to complete it as early as possible.

Motivate yourself by gratifying yourself that the day dreaming could be done another time and right now, the concentration over the topic is more important rather than making the strategies for achieving future success.

AIMLESS AND ABRUPT THOUGHTS

The aimless and abrupt thoughts are like the alarm bells when putting every effort in understanding and learning the topic. Suddenly, start thinking about the irrelevant thing and step ahead on the unrelated path are the common mistakes which we do in everyday living. But if this becomes serious issue and willing to get rid of it then try to be back at the point where you end up your concentration and limit yourself on focusing the topic.

CONFUSIONS AND VAGUE

While reading a book, confusions may occur and it will make distractions in the concentration of the topics or conversations. Some people start irrelevant conversation or may give you the entirely different answer in response to the question, it is due to the previous confusions would interrupt in replying the questions or the mind is not present over there, thus getting not a single point.

Vagueness in very common in studying the difficult and time consuming topic; for dealing with these attributes, the will power is important and try to encourage yourself to keep concentration in tempo.

SELF DOUBTS

Some people don't keep trust and believe in themselves and ultimately find difficulty in every task. Usually they end up like saying I can't do this, this is really difficult for me, am I able to do this? So, all these sentences show the lacking of confidence of achieving any task. A large numbers of individuals are also found who starts worrying before the exams or presentations; the result is self doubt and eventually, concentration power impaired thus facing the failures in the targeted tasks.

"Recently study was conducted in the California University that the distractions usually start after the 15 minutes of focus and the major culprits were smart phones and laptops."

Chapter 4 – WAYS TO IMPROVE THE CONCENTRATION

In the previous chapters, the discussion was about the cause of the low concentration power and influence of surroundings at the concentration. Now, the discussion is about the solution and strategies to cope out with the problem of concentrations. The ways are endless and it is totally depends on the person's will to improve himself. These ways are like the mind amplifiers and tools to maximize the concentration power when dealing with any situation successfully.

Our mind is reluctant to put some more effort in pursuing and learning new things, encouraging yourself for learning ways to sharpen the brain and improve the concentration ability would be the priority to acquire the definite success in your lives. Continuous exercising and practicing would be the main brain boosters when competing with the concentration improvisation trainings.

IMPROVIZATION THROUGH DIET

Adding smart foods and memory friendly drinks in your diet is the first step to enhance the concentration skill. All individuals must include the following foods in the daily routine.

GET A CUP OF COFFEE

Caffeine is not about merely relaxing agent but it can also help in the enhancement of the concentration and attention. University of Illinois found that the individuals, who drink a cup of coffee a day, can easily concentrate in the noisy area than the quiet room.

CHEWING A GUM

Gum chewers actually constantly increase the blood flow to the brain areas that are responsible for concentration and as a result, the concentration skill is also enhanced. Jaw is also exercised and thus giving an extra effect to your jaw muscles.

EAT CITRUS FRUITS

Sugar is the fuel of our body and we all need it even for doing a simple task. Citrus fruits like oranges are a great source of energy and will raise the level of concentration prolonging the attentiveness period.

DRINK NATURAL JUICES

Naturally extracted juices are the best helpers to increase the power of attention. Although, the effect is short term boost to memory, thinking and mental ability but the natural juices are enriched with the nutrients and minerals that energize the body.

NUTS AND SEEDS

Nuts and seeds contain the same natural stimulants like the caffeine and it also raises the concentration skill.

BLUEBERRIES AND AVACADOS

Blueberries protect the brain and contain the special nutrients which amplify the ability to focus on an object whereas the avocados help in the prevention of plaques and enhance blood flow leading to the precise attention to the object.

PROTEIN RICH MEAT

Protein diet including fish and other seafood is enhancing the fixing power to any target. Eating protein rich diet frequently could also augment the focus ability, thinking power and analyzing skill. This diet will also help in preventing the obesity.

IMPROVIZATION THROUGH INTERESTING TACTICS

The tactics are many and wide in range and if implemented, the results will be satisfactory as well as amazing. By applying different tactics and strategies to enhance the memory and focusing ability, the person's information processing will speed up. Excellent tactics are elaborated to cope with the low concentration power.

GET ADEQUATE AMOUNT OF SLEEP

Sleep should be proper and adequate to deal with the daily routine's concentration oriented tasks. If sleep isn't proper; then, you can't be attentive at your desired targets.

MAKE A PLAN

Planning has always been the helper of catching the targets on expected time. Make a proper plan featuring the time table and synchronization of the routine.

DO ONE THING AT ONE TIME

Try to convince your brain to complete one task at one time. Don't put burden of tasks upon you, avoid too much stuff and concentrate on one object and finish it first, then jump on the other.

APPLY THE '5 MORE' TECHNIQUE

It is the technique based on the 5 number either it is about reading or concentration. While reading a book or attending a boring seminar, tell yourself to read or attend it for more minutes with full concentration. It will enhance the focusing strength definitely.

GRAB THE RELEVANT KEYWORDS

Sometimes, it happens that you remember only particular word of the topic and conversation; this is good because keywords help in tracking the root of the topic and resultantly, you pick up the main topic or object.

OPT FOR THE CONCENTRATION FRIENDLY PLACES

Go to the library or study lounges to properly place the concentration and fix it over the targeted task.

DIVIDE THE TASK

Divide the task in consecutive breaks for accomplishing in a better manner. The greater the tasks divided the greater assistance in focusing as well as concentrating over the topic will be achieved.

LEARN FROM OTHER PEOPLE WHILE CONCENTRATING

Learn from other people, how they can efficiently do their work along with handling many tasks in their lives. Take inspiration from them and encourage yourself to increase the concentration ability.

START MUTTERING

This is really crazy and you might look mad while implementing this strategy but the effect is amazing. University of Thessaly in Greece conducted a study and revealed that the self talking needs more concentration and effort rather than reading the topic quietly.

ENJOY THE WITTY AND HUMORUS TOPICS

Engage yourself in watching TV or reading the humorous books. This will also help in increasing the concentration skill as well as relaxing your mind from stresses.

COLOR THERAPY WOULD BE GOOD TRY

University of Columbia concluded that the red color improves the concentration power and focus ability. If this fails then green color is the next best color to help you in enhancing the memory and fixing your focus on one point. Add red or green color in your room and include concentrate booster colors in your wardrobe.

USE TIMERS AND IMPLEMENT IT

Timer setting is the advance strategy and it eventually restricts you at the target along with the intention of achieving it in a limited duration of time.

TAKE DEEP BREATH AND STIMULATE THETA WAVES

Deep breathing will stimulate the special theta waves in your brain and it turns on the concentration zones of the brain.

IMPROVIZATION THROUGH EXERCISES

The enhancement is not only through the diet and modified tactics but some exercises are solely designed to amplify the memory and concentration skill.

- Sit on a chair with eyes close and count the minutes while observing how you can sit still on a chair for 5 minutes. Remember the surroundings should be quiet and calm.

- Fix your gaze on your outstretched finger for 5 minutes

- Fix your focus on an outstretched hand for 5 minutes

- Open and close the fist continuously for 5 minutes and concentrate on it properly.

- Make two marks on the mirror with the level of your eye and suppose them two human eyes are staring at you and you have to face them confidently. Do this for 5 minutes and concentrate on it.

- Concentrate on the wall clock while keeping yourself as comfortable as you can for 5 minutes.

BONUS TRICK

For convincing yourself and trying to concentrate fully on the topic, this bonus trick will help you out to get success in training your mind. WPMAI is the strategy that'll effectively and efficiently improves the concentration ability and sharpens the memory.

- W

Rule out the issues that are creating hurdles in targeting the object attentively. Ask yourself what the problem is? What are the factors which letting the concentration down and altered?

- P

Pick up the strategy for improving the concentration. Ask yourself what are the most useful strategies to deal with? How many options do I have?

- M

Motivate and convince your mind to try the strategy and see the results. Ask yourself can I do this? Will this help me out to minimize the concentration losing problem?

- A

Attempt the strategy to get the ultimate success of the exercising. Ask yourself what essentials do I need to start up the strategy?

- I

Inspection of the strategy's result and success is the last step of this trick. Ask yourself how effective is the strategy? Is the strategy worked for maximizing the concentration power? Should I give a try to other strategies as well?

Chapter 5 – RELATION OF CONCENTRATION ENHANCEMENT WITH THE EXERCISE AND MEDITATION

Knowing your lacking and deficiency is good aspect but doing nothing for solving the problem is the worst part. It'll lead you towards more deterioration than the correction of the issue but nowadays, the most popular method of increasing the power to fix on one target is the maximum utilization of exercise and meditation. Exercise and meditation merely is not a helper to reduce weight but it is also the complete energizer for your whole body's vital organs including brain.

If brain is sharp and smart then the focus will ultimately builds up and concentration is more enhanced to some extent. According to the Dr. John Ratey, associate clinical professor of psychiatry at Harvard Medical School '*by regular exercise and meditation, brain derived neurotrophic factor is released to boost up the memory areas and augments the memory, concentration and mental sharpness*'. So, exercise and meditation, both are the modified way of increasing the concentration and raising the memory.

YOGA AND AEROBICS

Your body needs relaxation after doing long hours work and to properly concentrate on another task. Yoga and aerobics are fun loving exercises; it'll stimulate the memory specified areas and improving the strength of concentration.

HIGH INTENSITY WORKOUTS

High intensity exercises increase the brain volume and increase the blood flow to the brain enhancing the ability to fix all the thoughts in one direction or the target.

FEEL YOUR BREATHING

Listen to your breathing while sitting still in a comfortable place closing your eyes for some minutes. Focus on your breathing and let the other thoughts fade. As a result, your entire focus is on the breathing and other thoughts will be vanished from your mind. Open the eyes when full concentration is achieved.

SAY PAUSE TO YOURSELF

Sit still on the mat after feeling your breath and close the eyes. And just focus on not moving a single inch. Try to maintain the focus until the other set of thoughts are fading away and then slowly open the eyes, after achieving focus on only one target at one time.

MANTRA TECHNIQUE

Close the eyes and say 'ohm' for the introduction of vibratory sensations in your body. While repeating the word ohm, exhale the air and when inhaling, try to abate the distracting thoughts. Mantra is the phrase which is repeated again and again in the meditation session. This helps in the development of concentrating even in an interrupted environment.

ACCELERATING THE MULTI TASKING ABILITY

It is thought that yoga and meditation at least one time a day can accelerate the ability to handle multiple tasks at one time smartly. So, mindfulness training could do wonders while carrying different activities and performing interesting tasks efficiently and effectively. Meditation would never be left, if you want to do the multitasking and defeat the lacking of your concentration.

" Oregon State University published a research that the 15 minutes of exercise improves the concentration as well as behavior."

Conclusion

In the end, I am in great debt of your attention and interest in paying to this text. Besides gratitude and pleasure, this summary won't enough to complete the diversity of the topic in some few words but the things could be changed by initiating first step for competing with the world confidently and efficiently.

We would be contended, when readers utilize this book and adopt the enlisted maneuvers in their daily living for combating with the issue of low concentration power. If you are unable to focus on the study and facing high failures in your academic journey then this guidebook will help to pull you out and change the failures into the triumph. Sometimes, diverted concentration also embarrasses you in front of the audience; this book also reveals the basic facts to deal with. The techniques are assembled and explained in a way to provide you the best possible procedure to remove the dearth of concentration power.

I hope that through this eBook, you'll definitely overwhelm the low concentration power and got the victory in all types of conversations, studies and meetings. So, concentration is a must have part of our lives, we all are incomplete without it. To get a grip on any target, concentration is the first stride among the other actions.

Thank you for reading. I hope you enjoy it. I ask you to leave your honest feedback.

Printed in Great Britain
by Amazon